ELT **Development Series**

SERIES EDITOR Thomas S. C. Farrell

Reflection-As-Action in ELT

Thomas S. C. Farrell

tesolpress

www.tesol.org/bookstore

TESOL International Association
1925 Ballenger Avenue
Alexandria, Virginia, 22314 USA
www.tesol.org

Director of Publishing and Product Development: Myrna Jacobs
Copy Editor: Sarah Duffy
Cover: Citrine Sky Design
Interior Design & Layout: Capitol Communications, LLC

ISBN 978-1-945351-39-6
Library of Congress Control Number 2018958334

Contents

Series Editor's Preface

The English Language Teacher Development (ELTD) Series consists of a set of short resource books for ESL/EFL teachers that are written in a jargon free and accessible manner for all types of teachers of English (native, non-native, experienced and novice teachers). The ELTD series is designed to offer teachers a theory-to-practice approach to second language teaching and each book offers a wide variety range of practical teaching approaches and methods of the topic at hand. Each book also offers time for reflections for each teacher to interact with the materials presented in the book. The books can be used in pre-service settings or in in-service courses and can also be used by individual looking for ways to refresh their practice.

Reflection-As-Action in ELT by Thomas S.C. Farrell explores how reflective practice can be operationalized in ELT and how such an approach can inform language teaching. As Farrell discusses this is not a 'why' or 'what' of reflective practice (see his earlier book: Farrell, T. S. C. (2013). *Reflective teaching.* Alexandria, VA: TESOL International Association); rather this is a 'how' to implement reflective practice book. The author outlines in detail with lots of activities, exercises and examples how language teachers can reflect using his five stage framework for reflecting on practice: philosophy, principles, theory, practice and beyond practice. *Reflection-As-Action in ELT* is another valuable addition to the literature in our profession and to the ELTD series.

I am very grateful to the authors who contributed to the ELTD Series for sharing their knowledge and expertise with other TESOL professionals. It is truly an honor for me to work with each of these authors as they selflessly gave up their valuable time for the advancement of TESOL.

Thomas S. C. Farrell

Introduction

How Can We Know the Dancer From the Dance?

("Among School Children," W. B. Yeats)

"Reflection" has become a buzzword in the field of teaching English to speakers of other languages (TESOL) and many other professions as a mark of professional competence, and, indeed, it is difficult to find any teacher education program that does not refer to this interesting, yet complex, concept (Farrell, 2018). However, when it comes to implementing or operationalizing reflection, teachers and teacher educators must choose from a vast array of different approaches, usually from within the field of general education rather than TESOL, with different theoretical backgrounds that can lead to confusion about what approaches are best for TESOL teachers. Indeed, this became especially true for me recently when I was asked to participate at the Chicago 2018 TESOL Convention as a distinguished TESOLer in the Tea With Distinguished TESOLers (http://www.tesol.org/convention-2018/ticketed-events/tea-with-distinguished-tesolers) on the subject of "Reflective Practice for Language Teachers." As I sat at the table with 10 teachers and teacher educators, the most common questions I got were "How do I implement reflective practice individually or with other teachers in a school/institution?" and "How do I use this for teacher evaluation or measure it?" Most participants said that they know what reflective practice is in essence, but that they do not really know how to implement it in their daily lives as teachers and/or teacher educators within the field of TESOL. I decided to write this book in the English Language Teacher Development (ELTD) series because I have recently developed a framework for operationalizing reflective practice for TESOL teachers using a holistic and comprehensive approach which, as you will read, offsets some of the shortcomings of other reflective approaches in the field of general education (Farrell, 2015).

From the outset, then, I would like to point out that this book is not about *what* reflective practice *is* or *why* it should be implemented, as I have addressed these questions in an earlier book in the ELTD series (see Farrell, 2013). This book can be viewed as a companion to that book, or a Part 2, as it addresses the question I get most: How can I implement (or operationalize) reflective practice? The "I" here refers to teachers, teacher educators, supervisors, administrators, and other stakeholders interested in implementing reflective practice.

The structure of the book is as follows: Chapter 1 outlines how reflective practice can be implemented in TESOL. Chapters 2 to 6 detail each of the five stages with examples of how one novice female English as a second language (ESL) teacher reflected at each level of the framework so that you can consider her reflections when composing and analyzing your own. Before reading on, however, ask yourself whether you are a reflective teacher.

REFLECTIVE BREAK

Zeichner and Liston (1996, p. 6) suggest five key features of a reflective teacher. Look at these features and assess how closely you follow, or do not follow, each of them and comment on each one. A reflective teacher

1. examines, frames, and attempts to solve dilemmas in classroom practice.

2. is aware of and questions the assumptions and values they bring to teaching.

3. is attentive to the institutional and cultural contexts in which they teach.

4. takes part in curriculum development and is involved in school change efforts.

5. takes responsibility for their own professional development.

CHAPTER 1

Reflection-As-Action

Introduction

For language teachers, reflective practice generally means systematically examining their beliefs and practices about teaching and learning throughout their careers. In a previous book, I outlined and discussed the "what" and "why" of reflective practice by suggesting four main principles: It is evidence-based, involves dialogue, links beliefs and practices, and is a way of life (Farrell, 2013). These four principles still hold true. I suggested that reflective practice is **evidence-based** because it involves teachers systematically gathering information (or data) about their practice and then using this information to make informed decisions. This principle remains a prominent part of the implementation of reflective practice. I also noted that reflective practice **involves dialogue** either with educators themselves as individuals (internal dialogue) or, even better, with other teachers (critical friends, team teaching, group discussions), because the collaborative process of dialoguing bolsters reflection. This dialoguing principle is also very important as teachers implement reflective practice. Moreover, I suggested that reflective practice **links beliefs and practices** when teachers examine what occurs (theories-in-use) in their practice and compare this to their beliefs (espoused theories) about learning and teaching. This remains true when implementing reflective practice, but the framework adds reflecting on philosophy, principles, and theory to practice and beyond practice, as you will read later. In addition, I noted that reflective practice is **a way of life** because it implies a dynamic way of being inside and outside the classroom. As teachers implement reflection throughout the framework, this principle becomes very important in reflecting in, on, and, for action because teachers construct and reconstruct their own theories of practice throughout their careers.

These principles still pertain to this book on how to implement reflective practice. In this chapter specifically, I outline and discuss how teachers can implement reflection through a five-stage framework (Farrell, 2015). The chapters that follow outline each of the five stages in more detail.

REFLECTIVE BREAK

What is your understanding of each of the four principles?

- *Principle 1*: Reflective practice is evidence based.
- *Principle 2*: Reflective practice involves dialogue.
- *Principle 3*: Reflective practice explores beliefs and practices.
- *Principle 4*: Reflective practice is a way of life.

Reflection-*As*-Action

One of the persistent issues still unresolved concerning reflective practice is how teachers and programs can implement or operationalize reflection (Freeman, 2016). Within TESOL, as Freeman (2016) recently agreed, reflection offers a way into the less "accessible aspects of teacher's work" (p. 208); he also notes that the level of access actually depends on how reflection is operationalized or implemented. In the field of general education, many different conceptualizations, approaches, and frameworks for implementing reflective practice have been proposed. However, careful scrutiny reveals that many of these approaches and frameworks tend to restrict reflection to a retrospective activity and to focus solely on problems in the classroom.

This retrospective approach, or as Freeman (2016) calls it, "post-mortem reflection" (p. 217), usually consists of asking questions (such as what?, why?, now what?) that limit the focus to reflection-as-repair to solve or fix some perceived problem in a type of "reflection bubble."

Although such retrospective approaches may offer structured ways into reflection, especially for novice teachers, the danger exists that reflection can become ritualized, mechanical, and even prescriptive by reducing it to a set of recipe-following checklists and questions for teachers. These defeat the original goal of reflective practice as it reappeared in the early 1980s of avoiding such technical rationality. The "reflection bubble" I mentioned previously produces gaps between the teacher doing the reflecting, the problem perceived, and the act of reflection itself. In other words, the perceived problem to be solved is "out there," away from the person-as-teacher. Just as we cannot know the dancer from the dance—they cannot be separated—I believe the teacher cannot be separated from the act of teaching. Thus, we also cannot separate the teacher-as-person from the perceived problem or the process of reflecting.

This gap in the reflective process can be removed by considering reflection-*as*-action, where the reflective process includes "awareness of the self, the context as well as the problem to be solved" (Bleakley, 1999, p. 323). Viewing reflection-*as*-action includes the teacher-as-person in a more holistic approach to reflective practice. Recently, I developed one such holistic approach to reflective practice for TESOL teachers that not only focuses on the same intellectual, cognitive, and metacognitive aspects of reflection as many other approaches do (and limit themselves to), but also includes reflection on the spiritual, moral, and emotional noncognitive aspects of reflection (Farrell, 2015). Thus, this framework acknowledges the inner life of teachers. The framework has five different stage of reflection: philosophy, principles, theory, practice, and beyond practice (see Figure 1). I'll explain each of these in more detail in the chapters that follow.

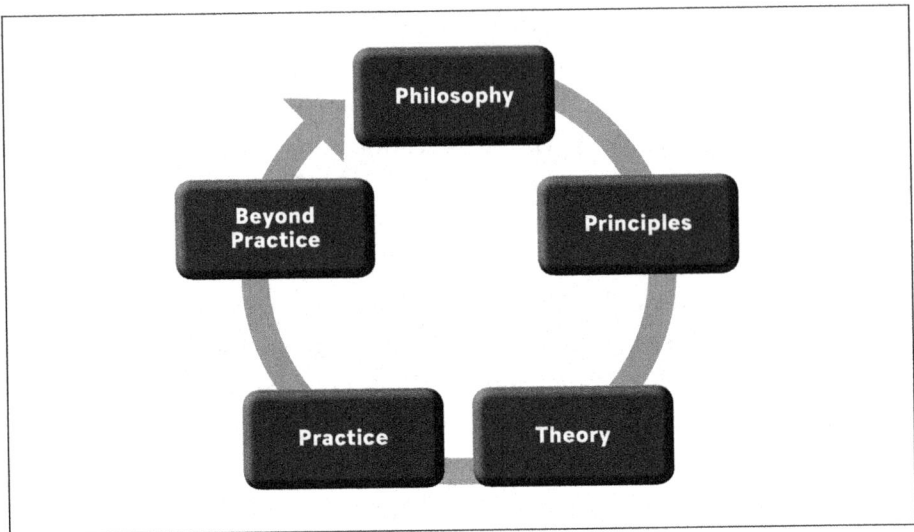

Figure 1. Framework for Reflecting on Practice (adapted from Farrell, 2015)

REFLECTIVE BREAK

What is the value of including the inner lives of teachers in the reflection process?

Figure 1 illustrates the framework as a circle, which can be navigated in three different ways: theory-into-practice, practice-into-theory, or single-stage application. Thus, the framework is descriptive rather than prescriptive. Teachers can take a deductive approach to reflecting on practice by moving from theory-into-practice or from stage 1, philosophy, through the different stages to stage 5, beyond practice. Some may say that preservice teachers with little classroom experience would be best suited to take such an approach because they can first work on their overall philosophical approach to TESOL and work their way through the different stages. They can begin with principles (stage 2) and move on to theory (stage 3); when they reach the practicum stage, they will be well placed then to reflect on their practice (stage 4); and eventually move beyond practice (stage 5).

- Do you think teachers can begin their reflections at any stage, or do you think they should begin reflecting on their philosophy of practice and then move to the next level and so on?

- At which stage of the framework would you like to begin your reflections and why?

- How would you like to move through the different stages of reflection outlined in the framework: theory-into-practice or practice-into-theory or some other movement?

Conclusion

This chapter suggests that the usual retrospective approaches to implementing reflective practice are too narrow because they omit the teacher-as-person from the process of reflection. However, viewing the process from the perspective of reflection-*as*-action grounds it in the belief that teachers are whole persons and reflection is multidimensional, thus including the social, political, moral, and spiritual. The chapter proposes that such an approach to implementing or operationalizing reflective practice for TESOL teachers can be accomplished through a framework with five stages: philosophy, principles, theory, practice, and beyond practice. As the chapters that follow indicate, throughout this reflective practice process, I encourage teachers at each stage not only to reflect but also to examine and challenge their embedded assumptions.

CHAPTER 2

Reflecting on Philosophy

Introduction

In the previous chapter, I introduced a framework for reflecting on practice that operationalizes reflective practice for language teachers. The framework has five main stages, and the first of these is philosophy. This chapter outlines and discusses how teachers can reflect on this first stage.

Reflecting on Philosophy

This first stage of operationalizing and implementing reflection within the framework examines the teacher-as-person and suggests that a teacher's sense of self and identity that originated at birth and continues to develop throughout life invariably guides professional practice, both inside and outside the classroom (Farrell, 2018). As Goodson (2000) maintains, "In understanding something so intensely personal as teaching it is critical we know about the person the teacher is" (p. 16).

Thus, reflecting on philosophy helps teachers gain self-knowledge by exploring, examining, and reflecting on their life history, or the place from which they evolved, and this includes their heritage, ethnicity, religion, socioeconomic background, and family and personal values. Obtaining such self-knowledge (sometimes overlooked in the literature on reflective practice) is important for teachers and their teaching because it allows them to construct their narratives of the self; as Palmer (1998) notes, "Good teaching requires self-knowledge. . . . Whatever self-knowledge we attain as teachers will serve our students and our scholarship well" (p. 3). Such a process can help teachers develop and nurture their personal and professional identities and close any gap between their expected teacher identities and their actual teacher identities.

REFLECTIVE BREAK

- Novice teachers can consider the following questions related to their identity development:
  - What are desirable qualities or abilities of a "good" TESOL teacher?
  - Who do you imagine yourself to be in the future as a TESOL teacher?
  - What teacher roles both inside and outside the classroom do you think you will perform when you begin teaching?
  - Can you think of any past experiences you had as a student that will impact you as a teacher?

- Experienced teachers can consider the following questions (adapted from Brookfield, 2006):
  - What are you proudest of in your work as a teacher?
  - What would you like your students to say about you when you are out of the room?
  - What do you most need to learn about in your teaching?
  - What do you worry most about in your work as a teacher?
  - What's the mistake you've made and learned the most from?
  - What are desirable qualities or abilities of a "good" TESOL teacher?

Reflecting on Teacher Identity

When TESOL teachers reflect on their philosophies, research indicates that they mostly focus on their identities (origins and development) as teachers (Farrell, 2018). Indeed, one particular study (Kanno & Stuart, 2011) suggests that TESOL teacher learning is not so much acquiring the knowledge of language-teaching methodology and skills as it is developing a teacher identity. This study also argues that the acquisition of knowledge (content knowledge and pedagogical knowledge) is part of this identity development, but not the other way around. In some instances, such reflection raises the possibility that an identity gap will develop between teacher identity expectations during preservice training and the reality of practice, and, as such, identity is always shifting (Liu & Xu, 2011). Thus, by being encouraged to engage in reflective practice, TESOL teachers begin to notice the gap, and, as a result, shift their identities (especially when identities compete) to adapt to different situations based on many rounds of reinterpretation of the self and the situation.

In addition, research indicates that context influences identity construction and development, which can shift as context changes (Kong, 2014). Thus, it is important to encourage teachers to become aware of the possibility of shifting identities. For TESOL teachers who change contexts, such as moving to a country different from their place of origin to study and/or work, the idea of shifting identities becomes even more important, and language teacher education programs can help teachers reflect on these possibilities. As Kong (2014) notes, teacher education programs can "provide reflective activities to help pre-service TESOL teachers understand and cope with the shifting of identity that will inevitable occur" (p. 91). The following section provides various reflective activities that teacher education and development programs can provide to help teachers access their philosophies. Teachers at all levels of experience can also practice these activities on their own or with others.

Accessing Philosophy

To access philosophy, teachers reflect on how they got where they are at present and how their past experiences influenced the various decisions they have made. One way for teachers to explore their philosophies is through autobiographical storytelling (Farrell, 2015). Teachers can reflect by constructing (either writing or telling, but both together would be best) in-depth autobiographical stories that cover the most important events in their lives from birth to the present. By reflecting in such a chronological manner, teachers can gain an understanding of who they are as persons and teachers and of their identity formation and development over time. Two such tools for reflecting on philosophy are the "tree of life" and narrative frames.

The tree of life (see Figure 2) visually represents a teacher's chronological development and represents their personal history from early experiences growing up, to those of today, either as an experienced teacher or a teacher-in-training. The tree of life is divided into *roots*, *trunk*, and *limbs* as follows:

- *Roots*: The roots provide the foundations of what shaped early years, such as family values, heritage, ethnicity, religion, and socioeconomic background.

- *Trunk*: The trunk captures experiences from early school years all the way to high school and university years; in other words, educational experiences as a student.
- *Limbs*: The limbs represent all professional experiences as a teacher.

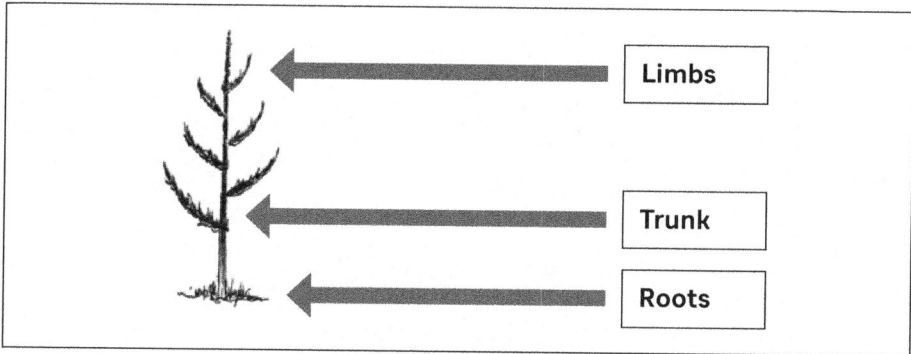

Figure 2. Tree of Life

After drawing their trees of life, teachers can begin to see particular prior experiences and events (both positive and negative) as being significant for their development as people and later as teachers. They can thus begin to identify and synthesize various life events, such as early childhood experiences; experiences as students in primary school; experiences as students in high school; experiences as students in college or university; any informal learning experiences; perhaps best/worst language learning experiences; best/worst courses/teachers; influential teachers as role models; best/worst teaching experiences. When teachers note all of these and more, they can begin to write up their stories to uncover past influences on their current teaching practice.

As mentioned, teachers can reflect on their philosophies by articulating in-depth autobiographical stories; however, such activities rely very much on memory, which can be selective. So teachers can also reflect on their pasts using a template to ease the vagaries of memory. Such guided activities may help teachers to focus on those experiences that play the biggest roles in their practice. One such activity is using "narrative frames," story templates consisting of incomplete sentences to be completed by the storyteller. These can in fact be closely linked with the results of the tree of life.

REFLECTIVE BREAK

Keeping in mind all the experiences in your life that have made you who you are, complete the following narrative frames (adapted from Farrell, 2015):

1. I became a teacher because . . .

2. When I first started to teach, I . . .

3. The place where I teach now is . . .

4. My students are . . .

5. I find teaching exciting and challenging because . . .

6. The best aspect of my life as a teacher is . . .

7. The worst aspect of my life as a teacher is . . .

8. When coming up with ideas for my classes, I usually think about . . .

9. I know I've done good work when . . .

10. I know I've done bad work when . . .

11. I feel best about my work when . . .

12. I feel worst about my work when . . .

13. The last time I saw really good teaching was when . . .

14. The best learning experience I've ever seen students involved in was when . . .

15. When I leave this school, my students and colleagues will remember me for . . .

Now, begin to try to connect the sentences into your story. What could be some of the life experiences that influenced how you completed these sentences? Ask yourself what type of teacher this story describes.

Here is an example of a novice ESL teacher's philosophy. After reading it, write your own philosophy.

I find that my philosophy of teaching stems primarily from my experiences as a second language learner and a novice teacher. My study of Japanese as a second language has been filled with ups and downs, good teachers and bad, positive experiences and negative ones. These have greatly influenced the way I think about teaching and the process of learning a second language. Furthermore, my first years of teaching were full of trial and error. However, making mistakes helped me gain insight into what teaching is all about. These reflections on my experiences both as a learner and teacher have helped me form the core of my philosophy of teaching.

I believe that a teacher's role is to encourage students to explore new worlds. I have strived to become fluent in the Japanese language and understand the culture. Along the way, I have met many people who have, in teaching me, opened doors I never knew were there and helped me expand my horizons. This is what I aspire to in my own teaching. I will never forget the day when one of my students stood up in class and explained that on her recent trip to Switzerland she had befriended a Swiss couple. With tears of happiness rolling down her face, she told me, "If it weren't for your class, it wouldn't have been possible." To me, this opening of doors is what language teaching is all about, and what makes it so worthwhile.

To be effective, teachers must teach the students, not the textbook. This means both being aware of students' needs, and having the skills, knowledge and flexibility to adapt the lesson plan where necessary. As a novice teacher, keeping to the textbook and following the directions of the teacher's book made me feel safe. However, once I started teaching junior high school students for entrance exams, I realized I could not just go through the motions. I had to ensure that they understood the content because their future educational path depended on their exam results. When some of my students started turning in homework full of errors, I decided I needed to change the way I taught. I started looking closely at what my students could and could not do and adjusting my teaching accordingly. Sometimes this entailed small group teaching to ensure each student was being taught to their needs, or presenting content in different ways if I felt students needed further clarification. This change in approach was reflected in my students' results. Every student passed their exams, and, on the basis of their English scores, was able to enter a top school. This prompted me to stop using the textbook as a crutch, and become more flexible in the way I taught. This flexibility was one of the reasons for my students' success and indeed my own: I received an A pass for the Cambridge Certificate in English Language Teaching for Adults (CELTA), with the tutors making particular comment on my ability to adapt the textbook to my students' needs. Teachers have a responsibility to their students to focus on learning, not teaching. Awareness of the students and the skill to adapt are the keys to teaching success.

My teaching philosophy is centered on these principles, which influence and reflect both how and what I teach. They originate from my relationships and experiences, and are coupled with a desire for my students to achieve the same success and satisfaction from second language learning as I have enjoyed. In my opinion, these philosophies are the key to building deep and lasting connections with students and making learning a stimulating and enjoyable experience for all.

Conclusion

Teachers can become more self-aware through telling their autobiographical stories, including accounts of who they are and how and why they decided to become teachers. When teachers reflect about their own lives and how they think their past experiences may have shaped the construction and development of their basic philosophies of practice, they will be able to critically reflect on their practice because they are more mindful and self-aware of their past. In summary, reflecting on their philosophies of practice can not only help teachers flesh out what has shaped them as human beings and teachers, but also help them move on to the next stage: reflecting on their principles.

CHAPTER 3

Reflecting on Principles

Introduction

In the previous chapter, I outlined and discussed how teachers can reflect on their philosophy. In this chapter, I outline and discuss how teachers can reflect on the second stage of the framework: principles.

Reflecting on Principles

When teachers reflect on their principles, they explore and examine their assumptions and beliefs about language teaching and learning. This level of reflection takes the process beyond the previous stage of person-as-teacher to include what teachers believe about teaching and learning English as a second or foreign language. These beliefs impact both their perceptions and judgments, and in turn affect their behavior in the classroom. However, teachers do not readily reflect on their beliefs, which often remain hidden and implicit. Because teachers' beliefs may or may not correspond to their practices, it is important for teachers to articulate their beliefs and achieve a level of awareness that enables them to reflect on whether these beliefs remain appropriate for their current practices. By self-reflecting on their beliefs, teachers can develop a deeper understanding of the origins of these beliefs, whether their practices reflect them, and vice versa. The next section addresses reflecting on teacher beliefs.

REFLECTIVE BREAK

- What are your assumptions about teaching and learning English to speakers of other languages?

- What are your beliefs about teaching and learning English to speakers of other languages?

- How do these beliefs influence your teaching?

- Where do your beliefs come from (sources of beliefs)?
    - Your past experience as a student
    - Your experience of what works best
    - Established practice in your school
    - Your personality
    - Research you read
    - Method(s) you follow
    - What do your learners believe about learning?
    - What do your learners believe about your teaching?

Reflecting on Teacher Beliefs

Kagan (1992) defines teacher beliefs as "tacit, often unconsciously held assumptions about students, classrooms, and the academic material to be taught" (p. 65). Articulation of such beliefs however, according to Abednia, Hovassapian, Teimournezhad, and Ghanbari (2013), permits TESOL teachers to better identify their teaching strengths and areas that need improvement and to gain the overall freedom to be able to continually modify existing beliefs whenever appropriate. Indeed, when TESOL teachers articulate their beliefs, they report feeling liberated because they can then better evaluate if these articulated beliefs are still appropriate in light of their new knowledge (Polat, 2010). However, research also indicates that TESOL teachers may struggle to articulate and externalize these tacitly held assumptions and beliefs, a common issue in the literature on teacher beliefs (Farrell, 2018). Assumptions and beliefs are not only difficult to articulate; some TESOL teachers also discover that once articulated, they are very complex and difficult to understand (Farrell & Bennis, 2013; Farrell & Ives, 2015). The following section provides various reflective activities that teacher education and development programs can use to help teachers access their principles. Teachers can adopt and practice these activities on their own as well.

REFLECTIVE BREAK

- How does articulating your underlying principles of teaching and learning enhance your reflections on their appropriateness for a particular context?

- Why do you think TESOL teachers may feel liberated as they become more aware of their principles of language teaching and learning?

- Why would some TESOL teachers struggle to externalize their underlying principles or have difficulty articulating their beliefs about teaching and learning?

Accessing Principles

Teachers can access their assumptions, beliefs, and conceptions in many ways. One way is to explore and examine them through teacher *maxims.* Teacher maxims usually derive from experience and guide teachers' instructional decisions; as such, they can also be considered rules for best behavior (Farrell, 2015).There are no correct or incorrect maxims, but reflecting on them can make teachers aware of their unconsciously held assumptions about teaching. The images these maxims, or personal working principles, produce become powerful introspective tools because teachers can use them as a lens to gain insight into their principles of practice.

REFLECTIVE BREAK

Examine the following list of maxims (from Farrell, 2015, pp. 54–56), and reflect on whether any apply to your own teaching situation:

- *Maxim of involvement:* Follow the learners' interests to maintain student involvement.
- *Maxim of planning:* Plan your teaching and try to follow your plan.
- *Maxim of order:* Maintain order and discipline throughout the lesson.
- *Maxim of encouragement:* Seek ways to encourage student learning.
- *Maxim of accuracy:* Work for accurate student output.
- *Maxim of efficiency:* Make the most efficient use of classroom time.
- *Maxim of conformity:* Make sure your teaching follows the prescribed method.
- *Maxim of empowerment:* Give the learners control.
- *Maxim of appropriate level:* Ensure students can perform tasks and not feel frustrated.
- *Maxim of flexibility:* Satisfy the needs of all types of learners.
- *Maxim of cooperation:* Encourage teacher-student, student-student, student-teacher group work.
- *Maxim of learner-centered class:* Elicit knowledge and help students acquire skills.
- *Maxim of cultural input:* Present cultural information in class.
- *Maxim of curiosity:* Design tasks to elicit and satisfy natural curiosity.
- *Maxim of independent learning:* Give instructions on independent learning.
- *Maxim of motivation:* Use tools for forming positive motivation.
- *Maxim of fallibility:* You are human and can make mistakes.
- *Maxim of self-esteem:* Students' self-confidence increases as they progress in the language.

Now think of one or two of your own maxims for language teaching. Explain these maxims and how they are your personal working principles.

Another means of assessing principles is by analyzing the *metaphors* teachers use to describe their practice. Teachers usually establish their metaphors before entering their teacher education programs and so should be brought to the level of awareness for teachers.

REFLECTIVE BREAK

The following activities can help you articulate and examine your metaphors.

- Complete the following sentence: "As a teacher, I am _____."

- What metaphor did you use for you as a teacher? Do you need to use more than one? If so, use as many as you like and try to explain the meaning of each.

- Has your use of metaphors changed over time since you became a language teacher? If yes, what differences have you noticed? What experiences have led to the change you noticed? If no changes have occurred in your metaphor usage, what experiences have resulted in this confirmation of your original metaphor usage?

- Examine the following teacher metaphors and discuss (a) their ranking and (b) if any apply to your teaching practice (from Lin, Shein, & Yang, 2012):
    - Nurturer
    - Cooperative Leader
    - Knowledge Provider
    - Artist
    - Innovator
    - Tool Provider
    - Repairer

As we conclude this reflection on principles, take a moment to clarify your beliefs about teaching and learning by exploring the following questions:

- What are my beliefs about teaching and learning?

- How do these beliefs influence my teaching?

Here is an example of a novice ESL teacher's principles. After reading it, write your own principles.

In reflecting on my principles, I have found a combination of metaphors and maxims which define my principles of practice and guide me as a teacher. These principles focus primarily on student-centered teaching, and are influenced by my experiences both as a second language learner and teacher.

I believe a teacher is like a gardener, and learners are the seeds that she tends. In order for a plant to grow, the gardener must know its particular characteristics and the kind of conditions in which it will thrive. She must feed it, water it, and provide it with the necessary care and attention for it to grow tall and strong. In the same way, a teacher must recognize the characteristics of the students she teaches—their abilities, learning styles, prior knowledge and experiences, and interests—in order to determine their optimal learning conditions. She feeds her students with knowledge; not so much as to overwhelm them, but not so little that they are unmotivated and unchallenged. Then she nurtures them so their knowledge grows, and provides opportunities for them to flourish.

This metaphor differs from the one I held when I first started teaching. Then, I believed that teachers were like tour guides, leading students through their learning, explaining the things they encountered and walking a path of ups and downs together with the students. However, through experience, I have realized that leading learners as a group in the same direction does not allow for learner differences. Some may want to stray from the path and explore different things, some may not be able to keep up, and others may want to run ahead. From my experience, it is more effective to look at the individual and consider how each student can be nurtured so they can reach their full potential. My style of teaching, therefore, is learner-centered. I teach students new language then give them opportunities to use the language through various tasks and activities. I monitor the students' language and interactions, provide support where necessary, and use my observations to help me determine how to further extend their knowledge and skills.

Conclusion

This chapter outlines and discusses opportunities for teachers to reflect on their principles, the second stage of the framework. When teachers articulate their principles of teaching using maxims, metaphors, and belief analysis, they can question their continuing applicability in light of new information (if not, they can make modifications) and begin to reduce any discrepancy between what they do and what they think they do. The following chapter implements reflection in the next stage in the framework: theory.

CHAPTER 4

Reflecting on Theory

Introduction

In the previous chapter, I outlined and discussed how teachers can reflect on their principles. In this chapter, I outline and discuss how teachers can reflect on the third stage of the framework: theory.

Reflecting on Theory

When teachers reflect on their theory, they become more aware of the different concepts and theoretical principles that underlie their instructional practices. For the purposes of this chapter, "theory" refers to the different choices teachers make about particular skills taught (or that should be taught) in their day-to-day lessons. As they reflect on their approaches and methods at this stage, teachers will also reflect on the specific teaching techniques they choose to use (or may want to use) and whether these are (or should be) consistent with the approaches and methods they have chosen or will choose. Of course, reflections on philosophy and principles as outlined in the previous chapters will influence teachers' consideration of theory. Teachers will need to access their theory by describing specific classroom techniques, activities, and routines that they are using or intend to use when carrying out their lessons. The next section addresses reflection on lesson planning.

Reflecting on Lesson Planning

Research indicates that as a result of engaging in collaborative lesson planning, TESOL teachers become more aware of their students' needs than their own needs (Shi & Yang, 2014). For example, Shi and Yang (2014, p. 138) examined the reflections of TESOL teachers in collective lesson-planning conferences for a writing course and discovered that "participants [in collaboration with others] were not only able to develop a shared understanding of lesson planning and by negotiating "their own views, make meanings applicable to new circumstances, to enlist the collaboration of others, [and] to make sense of events," but were also "able to get a better understanding of the links between their own theories and practices." In this manner, many studies highlight the use of collaborative lesson planning as a means of encouraging TESOL teachers to engage in such reflections, which enable them to identify important issues related to planning, to realize the possibility of different types of instruction, to propose specific actions to enable successful lessons, and to evaluate these in light of imagined classroom events (Farrell, 2018).

Exploring and examining critical incidents (inside and outside the classroom) can be used to guide teachers' theory building. A critical incident is any unplanned but clearly remembered event that occurs in class, outside class, or anytime during a teaching career (Farrell, 2015). However, incidents only really become critical when subjected to conscious reflection. When language teachers formally articulate and then analyze these critical incidents, they can uncover new understandings of their practice. The following section provides various reflective activities that teacher education and development programs can provide to help teachers access their theory.

REFLECTIVE BREAK

- How do you plan lessons?

- Do you use a set syllabus? If yes, who made it and how is it designed? If not, do you make your own syllabus? Daily, weekly, monthly, etc.

- Do you plan extensively (e.g., do you write detailed lesson plans)? If yes, what do you usually write? If no, why don't you write extensive plans?

- How do you plan the content you will teach? From the textbook and/or the syllabus?

- How do you plan and sequence activities?

- How do you plan your method and approach to teaching a particular lesson?

- Do you ever go into a lesson without planning?

Accessing Theory

To access theory at this stage of the framework, teachers are encouraged to reflect on their theoretical orientation to planning lessons, as well as on critical incidents (personal and teaching). Planning involves the complex task of thinking about suitable lesson content to teach and how to teach it, the appropriate methods and activities to use, and the lesson's desired outcomes. As they reflect on their approaches and methods at this stage, teachers will also reflect on the specific teaching techniques they choose to use (or may want to use) in their lessons and whether these are (or should be) consistent with the approaches and methods they have chosen or will choose. To reflect on these, they will need to describe specific classroom techniques, activities, and routines they are using or intend to use when conducting their lessons.

Three different lesson plan designs lie at the heart of the lesson-planning process and highlight different theoretical underpinnings for teaching languages. These are *forward*, *central*, and *backward* designs (see Ashcraft, 2014, for a full discussion). These three designs influence the direction in which a lesson develops, and teachers should be aware of what each involves. Generally, in forward planning, the teacher identifies the lesson content first and then decides on the particular teaching methods and activities to use to teach the content. In central planning, the teacher chooses specific teaching methods and activities first and then considers the content and outcomes of the lesson. In backward planning, the teacher considers the desired lesson outcomes first, or what students are required to know at the end of the lesson, as well as what type of evidence will be necessary to show that the desired learning has taken place.

REFLECTIVE BREAK

Consider these questions about the way you plan lessons:

- When planning lessons, do you begin by considering the *content* that you will be teaching first?

- When planning lessons, do you begin by considering the *methods* and *activities* that you will be teaching first?

- When planning lessons, do you do you decide on the desired *learning outcomes* first?

As mentioned above, teachers can access their theory by analyzing critical incidents both inside and outside the classroom. Critical incidents inside the classroom include any events to which critical significance can be ascribed. To analyze these incidents, teachers need to engage in reflective activities such as self-observation while teaching and/or inviting peers to observe their classes. Teachers can keep a record of these incidents in a teaching journal and/or use video and/or classroom observations. Classroom data for analyzing critical incidents include audio, video-action replays, and lesson transcripts (see the next chapter on reflecting on practice). Lesson transcripts can be made from audio or video clips of classroom events. Teachers can analyze why an incident happened at that moment and then decide why this incident led to a change in teaching.

REFLECTIVE BREAK

Try to answer the following questions about each critical incident:

- What was the incident in your class?

- Why was this incident important to you?

- What happened exactly in the lesson that made this event important?

- How did you react (did you react?) at the time of the incident?

- Did you stop teaching?

- What does this critical incident tell you about your beliefs and values as they relate to teaching?

Critical incidents also occur outside the classroom (I call these "personal critical incidents") and can include events that result in major changes in your professional life. Indeed, such an event may have led you to become a teacher. Your tree of life (see Chapter 2) can provide an overall view of what has influenced you as a teacher throughout your career. This knowledge may also help you figure out where you want to go as a teacher Try to answer the following questions (you can make use of your tree of life to help you):

- What critical incidents in your youth shaped you as a teacher?

- What critical incidents in your college days shaped you as a teacher?

- What critical incidents in your early teaching days shaped you as a teacher?

- Do you teach in reaction to any of these? Explain.

- What general critical incidents in your career shaped you as a teacher?

- Do you teach in reaction to any of these critical incidents?

Here is an example of a novice ESL teacher's theory. After reading it, write your own theory.

As a novice teacher, my planning followed forward design and lesson content was determined by the textbook and planning centered on methods of teaching this content. At the time, this was the only way I knew how to plan. However, as I grew in experience, forward planning was increasingly reserved for lessons for cram school students studying for school entrance examinations. In such classes, I had to synchronize lesson content with what the students were studying at school, ensuring they mastered the target language in preparation for their tests. Thus, planning for each lesson started by identifying the language the students needed to learn then considering effective ways of presenting it. From this, I determined lesson learning outcomes and assessment methods. I disliked planning in this way as it was textbook- rather than student-centered. However, forward planning helped me cover the content the students needed to learn and ensure their understanding was sufficient to enable application to different exam questions. As a result, all of my students performed well in their English exams.

As I grew more confident and began focusing on students' learning rather than my own teaching, I found myself increasingly employing backward planning; determining first what I wanted students to achieve then planning how this could be accomplished. I found this method useful for all classes as it moved the planning focus from textbook content to the learners' needs while facilitating the forging of connections between new learning and prior knowledge. I determined students' needs by conducting needs analyses, formative assessment, and post-lesson reflections, then found, adapted, and presented content to meet these needs.

In classes where I was not curriculum-bound and had more freedom in what I taught, I occasionally used central planning for lessons. These classes were aimed at adult students studying English for overseas travel and communication purposes. As no curriculum existed, I could make lessons activity-based, and consequently encourage the students to freely express themselves, scaffolding and supporting each other while taking more control of their learning.

When planning, I looked for activities that would allow students to apply their language knowledge in different contexts and facilitate the sharing of language and strategies. After finding a suitable activity, I would then consider the language I needed to teach and methods of student assessment.

In examining how I plan for teaching, I have seen that my theory of practice centers on adaptation to the needs and situations of my students. These needs are varied, as is my role as teacher. For students studying for exams, I must ensure a thorough understanding of textbook content and the accurate use and application of target language. Conversely for students studying communicative English, I must identify areas of focus, provide the support they require to meet their goals, and facilitate learner agency. Using combinations of central, forward, and backward planning has given me the flexibility to teach according to this theory of practice.

Conclusion

This chapter outlines how TESOL teachers can reflect on their theory, the third stage of operationalizing reflective practice. Reflecting on theory through lesson-planning analysis and critical-incident analysis enables them to build repertoires and knowledge of instruction. This stage of reflection prepares teachers to be able to reflect clearly on what they actually do in class, that is, on their practice. The following chapter moves implementation of reflection on to the next stage in the framework: practice.

CHAPTER 5

Reflecting on Practice

Introduction

In the previous chapter, I outlined and discussed how teachers can reflect on their theory. In this chapter, I outline and discuss how teachers can reflect on the fourth stage of the framework: practice.

Reflecting on Practice

Up to now, the framework has emphasized reflecting on philosophy, principles, and theory, the "hidden" (the invisible) aspects of teachers' work. Reflecting on practice (the visible) begins with an examination of observable actions while teaching as well as of students' reactions (or nonreactions) to what and how teachers teach during lessons. Of course, such observable actions are directly related to and influenced by teachers' reflections on their theory at the previous stage as well as their principles and philosophy. Teachers can scrutinize if and how their theoretical foundations (philosophy, principles, and theory) influence their practice and if and how their practice influences their theoretical foundations. Teachers can reflect while they are teaching a lesson (reflection-*in*-action) and/or after they teach a lesson (reflection-*on*-action). When teachers engage in reflection-in-action, they attempt to monitor and adjust to various circumstances happening within the lesson. When teachers engage in reflection-on-action, they examine what happened in a lesson after the event. However, reflection-on-action can also include some kind of anticipatory reflection, or reflection-*for*-action. Reflection-for-action can be a culmination of reflection-in-action and reflection-on-action, as teachers attempt to consider what will come next in light of what went before. The next section addresses reflection on instructional decisions teachers make before, during, and after lessons.

REFLECTIVE BREAK

- What kind of reflecting (if any) do you do immediately after teaching a class?

- Have you ever gathered data on your class and discussed your findings with a colleague teacher? If so, explain,

- A lesson is a dynamic event during which many things occur simultaneously. How can you hope to become aware of everything that is happening in your classrooms?

- Good and Brophy (1991) outline the following classroom problems that occur because a teacher lacks awareness of their own behavior in the classroom. Have you ever experienced any of these problems in your teaching? If yes, explain what happened and how you reacted.
    — Teacher domination
    — Lack of emphasis on meaning
    — Overuse of factual questions
    — Few attempts to motivate students
    — Not cognizant of effects of seat location and grouping
    — Overreliance on repetitive seatwork

- Try to think about your teaching while you teach. (Write down your thoughts at various times during the lesson if you get a chance.)

Reflecting on Instructional Decisions

Reflecting (through classroom observations mostly) on practice in combination with theory leads to enhanced awareness of theory and practice connections (Farrell, 2018). Yuan and Lee (2014) indicate that postobservation discussions with peers not only heighten teachers' awareness of connections between practice and the previous three stages (philosophy, principles, and theory), but such awareness can lead to changes in each stage because teachers will begin to experiment with different teaching approaches. Other research reports that TESOL teachers can become more aware of different instructional possibilities when some kind of feedback or guidance is provided in pre- and postobservation conferences or in peer groups because such feedback can function as a trigger for teacher reflection (Waring, 2014). As Waring (2014) suggests, when feedback is provided, the teacher, when accepting or rejecting, also reflects on their reasoning and considers alternative courses of action to continue or change approaches. The following section provides various reflective activities that teacher education and development programs can provide to help teachers access their practice.

REFLECTIVE BREAK

- Do you ever talk to other teachers after class about teaching? What do you talk about?

- Many studies suggest that some form of feedback or guidance from a mentor and/or peers may be important to foster critical reflection. Why is this?

- Many studies encourage peer-mentoring as a means of fostering sharing among TESOL teachers when reflecting on their practice and theory. Do you trust your peers to be able to give you appropriate feedback?

- Do you ever talk to students about their perceptions of your class and teaching? What do you talk about?

- Do you ever ask students to tell you what they think they learned in your class?

Accessing Practice

Teachers have several different methods of accessing their reflections on practice. For example, they can engage in classroom observations (self-monitoring, peer critical friendships, or group observations), and they can record (audio and/or video) their lessons and later transcribe the recordings for a more accurate recounting of what occurred. Teachers can also consider conducting action research on specific aspects of their practice if they think they need to improve some facet of their teaching or their students' learning.

REFLECTIVE BREAK

To engage in classroom observations and especially self-observation/monitoring, reflect on various aspects of your practice before, during, and after teaching. Here are some questions to consider *before* you teach a class:

- Do you start your classes the same way each day?

- Do you end your classes the same way each day?

- Do you follow textbooks by page numbers exactly (routinely)? If no, what do you with the prescribed textbooks you must use?

- Do you stand/sit in the same place during each class?

- Do you call on the same students to answer questions?

- Are the students required to raise their hands and wait to be nominated before asking or answering a question, or can they shout out and participate more spontaneously in your classes?

- What level of formality operates within your class?

- How and when are students expected to interact with other students?

- Can students move around the room whenever they want?

- If a student needs help with something, when and how does the student approach you?

- To what extent are your students free to challenge what you say?

Answering these questions will impart an awareness of what you think you do *while* teaching and how you plan for this. Now you are ready to "see" what you actually do during class by recording your lessons. However, given each lesson's complexity, it is a good idea to decide on some focus for your classroom observation before you begin to audio and/or video your lesson (we do this to have retrievable data). Make a list of topics in order of importance to focus on. Some examples might include

- How do you begin and end your classes?
- How do you give instructions? Are they clear? How do you know?
- How do you give feedback?
- How do you elicit answers from students?
- What is the proportion of teacher-talk to student-talk?
- What are your classroom management strategies? (Farrell, 2015, pp. 85–86)

Record your lesson. *After* reviewing the recording, try to answer the following questions:

- What did you do well?
- What did you not do so well?
- What did you learn about your teaching?
- How well did you do in relation to the following aspects?
  — Pacing
  — Explaining
  — Asking and answering questions: how many, what kind, to whom?
  — Giving feedback to students
  — Creating a positive and supportive atmosphere (Farrell, 2015, p. 86)
- Reflect on the different types of learners in your class from the following six types (adapted from Richards & Lockhart, 1994):
  — Task-oriented Learners
  — "Phantom" Learners
  — Social Learners
  — Dependent Learners
  — Isolated Learners
  — Alienated Learners
- Ask a peer to join you for classroom observations. Decide what aspects of your teaching you would like to look at and/or discuss.

Although many in TESOL tend to consider action research a stand-alone activity, it actually comes under the umbrella of reflective practice as Dewey (1933) originally initiated it when he outlined his theory of reflective inquiry. Dewey maintained that when teachers want to engage in reflective practice, one of the most important things they should first do is slow down the interval between thought and action by engaging in reflective inquiry that has five main phases:

1. *Suggestion*: The teacher understands a doubtful situation to be problematic and considers some vague suggestions as possible solutions.

2. *Intellectualization*: The teacher intellectualizes the difficulty or perplexity of the problem that has been felt (directly experienced) into a problem to be solved.

3. *Guiding idea*: The teacher collects factual material.

4. *Reasoning*: The teacher decides to implement actions but is not sure yet if they will work.

5. *Hypothesis testing*: The teacher tests and monitors this refined hypothesis. If successful, the teacher can draw strong positive conclusions about their solutions. If this fails, the teacher must try some other solution and see what happens.

This reflective inquiry cycle is very similar to action research procedures that have been proposed in general education and in TESOL. These general stages (cyclical) of the action research process are

- *plan* (identify problem),
- *research* (review literature),
- *observe* (collect data),
- *reflect* (analyze), and
- *act* (redefine problem).

Reflection-*As*-Action in ELT

REFLECTIVE BREAK

Decide on a topic you would like to investigate as an action research project. You can check all the topics of the ELTD series for ideas, but here are some examples that will help get you started (Farrell, 2015):

- *Teaching the skills* (issues related to changes in the way you teach aspects of reading, writing, listening, grammar, vocabulary, or speaking)

- *Classroom dynamics and grouping arrangements* (issues related to the kinds of interactions that occur in your language classroom or how different grouping arrangements, such as pair, group, or whole class, promote learner motivation, language use, and cooperation)

- *Learner language* (issues related to the kind of language generated by specific activities your students use when completing classroom discussions and the amount of language they produce during pair or group work)

- *Use of materials* (issues related to different ways you use materials and how these affect the outcomes of lessons)

- *Assessment policies and techniques* (issues related to the forms of assessment you currently use in your classes and their outcomes)

Decide on how you will collect information about the problem to be investigated. You can choose from several methods such as journals or diaries where you record accounts of teaching/learning plans, activities, and classroom occurrences, including your personal philosophy, principles, and theory of practice. You can also collect lesson plans, students' writings, classroom materials/texts, assessment tasks/texts, student profiles, and student records. You might engage in classroom (participant or nonparticipant) observations and take note of what actually occurs (and record the lesson). Of course, you can combine such observation with journal notes and recordings that can be transcribed in the places where the actual problem in practice occurs. Once the data have been collected, you can now begin to analyze and reflect on them and make a data-driven decision to take some action with the idea of problem redefinition: What have you learned from this focus and how have your redefined the problem?

Here is an example of a novice ESL teacher's practice. After reading it, write your own practice.

> One of the challenges I have faced in my teaching is catering to the disparate abilities of adult students in mixed level classes. A major priority, therefore, has been finding methods of teaching course content in ways that challenge, motivate, and engage all students, regardless of ability. Group work is a strategy I have often employed, and in an effort to encourage as much variety of interaction as possible, I have always grouped students at random. Although students seem to work well in this way, I am aware that new students sometimes feel intimidated by the more able learners. As this can potentially impact student motivation and participation, I wish to investigate groupings further focusing on two questions:
>
> 1. How do learners feel about homogeneous grouping (being grouped with classmates of similar levels) compared to heterogeneous grouping (being grouped with classmates of different levels)?
> 2. Do these different groupings affect the degree of student participation?
>
> This investigation would help me improve students' learning by enabling me to group them in ways that are most beneficial to them. It would also make me more aware of the dynamics of different groupings and their effects on the way students participate. This, in turn would influence the types of activities I choose for my lessons and the way I ask my students to interact.
>
> The study would be conducted in one of my smaller classes; a class of eight consisting of four beginner and four pre-intermediate students. This would allow me to create two groups which I can observe simultaneously and unobtrusively. Data would be collected through observation and student questionnaires. I would monitor student interaction over the course of two lessons; one using heterogeneous groupings and the other homogeneous. The observations would focus on students' communication and participation, any issues that arise, and how the students react to such issues. I would make written notes both as I observe and after each lesson in a reflective diary. Additionally, I would make audio

recordings and transcripts of the group interactions to assist me in analyzing the content of students' communication, and to determine their degree of participation. It is also important to listen to the voices of the students themselves. Questionnaires with a mixture of closed (Likert-scale) and open-ended questions would be used at the end of each lesson to garner feedback on group dynamics and student participation.

The observation notes would be used to examine general patterns of student interaction and participation. The recordings would be analyzed using a SCORE [seating chart observation record] chart to determine the frequency of utterances of all group members and hence the degree of each student's participation. Furthermore, students' language would be analyzed from the transcript by classifying the types of utterances made (e.g., question, explanation, suggestion, prompt, etc.). This would help determine whether groupings affect the nature of students' participation, for example, whether low-level students are more likely to ask questions when working in a heterogeneous group or in a homogeneous group. The answers to the Likert questionnaire items would be tabulated and mean scores calculated. These scores would be analyzed both separately and summed to ascertain students' feelings about each grouping. Finally, the answers to the open-ended questions would provide more detailed information to complement the Likert data. The data results from the two lessons would then be compared and contrasted in order to determine the differences in student participation, interaction, and response to the two types of grouping.

Studying the effects of different groupings on my students would help me create a learning environment in which my students can be comfortable, motivated, and productive. As many of my classes are multi-level, I could take the results of the study on this small group into consideration when planning for other classes. This would help me to make my classes even more student-centered, enabling me to align my teaching more closely with my philosophy and principles of practice.

Conclusion

Teachers do not teach in isolation from their personal philosophies, principles, or theory. However, for many years in TESOL, teaching methods took center stage, and both teacher educators and teachers focused on behavioral aspects of practice to the detriment of the person-as-teacher, and, of course, their philosophy, principles, and theory of practice. This chapter explores how teachers can systematically reflect on practice in combination with other stages in the framework. Reflecting on practice through classroom observations can be done by a teacher alone or with the aid of peers and/or mentors. When teachers reflect on their practice in combination with the previous three stages (philosophy, principles, and theory), they can develop new understandings and insights about their students, teaching, and themselves as teachers. Teachers can also conduct action research projects on issues that arise from classroom observations, and these projects can be directed to resolving classroom-based issues or expanded beyond the classroom. The following chapter moves implementation of reflection on to the fifth and final stage in the framework: beyond practice.

CHAPTER 6

Reflecting Beyond Practice

Introduction

In the previous chapter, I outlined and discussed how teachers can reflect on their practice (and in combination with philosophy, principles, and theory). In this chapter, I outline and discuss how teachers can reflect on the fifth and final stage of the framework: beyond practice.

Reflecting Beyond Practice

This fifth stage of the framework involves reflecting beyond the technical aspects of practice and thus takes on more sociocultural and moral dimensions related to TESOL as a profession. This is also sometimes called "critical reflection," and it entails exploring and examining the contemplative, reflective, cognitive, emotional, ethical, moral, social, and political issues that impact teachers' practice both inside and outside the classroom. Critical reflection moves teachers beyond practice and links practice more closely to broader sociopolitical as well as affective/moral issues that impact practice. Teachers' ability to transform the profession into something they consider equitable for all transforms reflection from technical to "critical." Teachers reflect beyond practice to be able to understand how particular societal assumptions they may have been following in practice are in fact socially restrictive. By engaging in critical reflection, teachers can develop new ideas that empower them to become transformative intellectuals within society. Consequentially, reflections beyond practice can increase TESOL teachers' awareness of the many political agendas and economic interests that can (and do) shape how language teaching and learning are defined. The next section addresses reflection related to issues beyond the classroom.

REFLECTIVE BREAK

- Do you think teachers should look beyond their practice and reflect on how they impact and are impacted by society?

- Have you ever faced dilemmas beyond practice such as
  — mandated and centralized curricula?
  — burdensome administration related to accountability demands?
  — limited interaction because of timetabling arrangements or physical location?
  — large classes and lack of resources?

- Do you think the TESOL profession as a whole engages in critical reflection?

Reflecting Beyond the Classroom

When TESOL teachers reflect beyond their practice in combination with the other stages (philosophy, principles, theory, and practice), research reports that they are not only able to reflect on their own assumptions, beliefs, and theories and how they could use this information to improve their practice, but also on how these are all connected to wider school and social issues within the community in which they practice (Farrell, 2018). Indeed, as one study noted, such critical reflection allows TESOL teachers to go beyond language instruction and fulfill educationally oriented promises such as helping people become critical thinkers and active citizens (Deng & Yuen, 2011). As Deng and Yuen (2011) note, such critical reflection on deeper social issues beyond practice leads to greater awareness of "social issues, inequitable relationships and generated roles," thus enhancing "their critical thinking as both teachers and learners" (p. 450). The following section provides various reflective activities that teacher education and development programs can provide to help teachers access critical reflection beyond practice.

REFLECTIVE BREAK

- Critical reflection involves a process of unearthing and identifying previously unquestioned norms in society, the community, the school, and the classroom within the contexts in which they are practiced. How can you go about this type of critical reflection?

- Do you think that TESOL teachers should be encouraged to take on the role of social agents to promote changes that impact their learners' lives? If yes, why and how? If no, why not?

Accessing Beyond Practice

TESOL teachers can become more aware of the impact of their practice on society, and the impact of society on their practice, by consciously engaging in critical analysis of various aspects of their profession. As a result of this type of reflection, teachers can begin to understand the power dynamics inherent in education (in the classroom and beyond) and to question the beliefs that may have been externally imposed on them.

REFLECTIVE BREAK

The following questions (adapted from Farrell, 2015) can guide you to reflect beyond the technical aspects of your practice.

- What are your views about power relations in your classroom, and where did they originate?

- Is there a noticeable rank order of staff at your school? If so, where do you think you rank and why?

- Does your school or office of education have policies in place to help differently abled students? If so, have you been informed of these policies and your place within them as an English language teacher?

continued on next page

(Continued)

- Have you ever been concerned about job security?

- If so, what prompted this concern?

- What actions did you take to try to protect your job, or did you not act to do so?

- Is collaboration with colleagues encouraged or discouraged?

- If it is discouraged, why?

- If it is encouraged, how is it encouraged and why?

- Does your status as a TESOL teacher affect your life inside and outside the classroom (positively or negatively)? If so, how do these effects emerge in your teaching practice?

- What links do you perceive between your morals and/or religious beliefs and your practice?

- Do you have any conflicts between your personal morals and anything in your work context: students, colleagues, materials, administrators?

Another way TESOL teachers can access beyond practice is to take a critical stance in the TESOL profession. Crookes (2009) offers one approach TESOL teachers can follow when taking a critical stance in the community (even when asking legislatures to help with funding) involving a set of four actions:

1. *Organize*: Develop institutional networks, develop connections with parents, and develop networks in the community.

2. *Address leadership*: Address leadership, but try to see that all are leaders if provided with the right orientation and skills.

3. *Fund-raise*: The literature on fund-raising in education targets mainly the postsecondary level and gives little other guidance.

4. *Engage in action*: The old slogan "direct action gets the goods" is relevant because, in many places, conventional politicking will not provide what a critical language teacher might need.

Follow these steps in your community to solve some injustice you perceive to be present for your students and/or your teachers.

One final aspect related to the concept of critical reflection is the consideration of TESOL teaching as a moral activity. In the TESOL profession, with so many publishers plying their trade on the hard-earned cash of English language students, many of whom are refugees, teachers must ask themselves what morals are present in and absent from the profession and themselves. Consider these questions about morals and the profession:

- Do you believe that TESOL teachers' conduct at all times and in all ways is a moral matter both inside and outside the classroom?
- Some scholars have argued that spiritual and religious beliefs should be part of academic conversations. Do you agree?

Here is an example of a novice ESL teacher's beyond practice. After reading it, write your own beyond practice.

A major issue in TESOL in some countries is that, despite the time spent on English teaching in schools, students' communicative skills remain poor. In an attempt to remedy this, there has been a trend towards starting English learning at increasingly younger ages. Today, many English language schools offer lessons to pre-school children and weekly English lessons are common in kindergartens. I taught children as young as two at such institutions. However, the absence of curricula, a dearth of appropriate teaching materials and extremely short lesson times led me to question the value of these classes.

The notion that earlier is better in second language (L2) learning stems from the precepts of the "Critical Period Hypothesis" (CPH) which asserts that the period up until puberty is optimal for language acquisition. Studies have shown that learners who start young are more likely to achieve fluency than those who start post-puberty. Proponents of early childhood English education have used these findings to justify their claims; this has in turn influenced the policies of educational institutions in establishing classes for younger learners. However research advocating the CPH describes the success of younger starters only in contexts where learners are immersed or receive substantial input in the L2. These benefits do not appear to translate to learners receiving classroom instruction whose L2 input is extremely limited by comparison. The pre-school lessons I taught were only twenty or thirty minutes long and took place just once a week. To claim benefits from such limited exposure using the CPH as justification is surely questionable. Advocates for starting early also argue that it enables greater and longer exposure to the L2 resulting in confidence and positive attitudes to language learning. While this may be true, it can be debated whether twenty minutes a week constitutes adequate L2 exposure. Literature that addresses the long term effectiveness of such short pre-school lessons is scarce.

Conclusion

This chapter presents the final stage of the framework for reflecting on practice: beyond practice or critical reflection for TESOL teachers. Critical reflection involves looking beyond the classroom to some of the social forces in play when teachers perform their work. Social forces and political trends heavily influence teaching as different types of discrimination may be inherent in different educational systems. In other words, no practice is without theory or ideology; every practice promotes some sort of ideology, and it is always best to be aware of this. Reflections at this stage can assist teachers in becoming more aware of the many political agendas and economic interests that can (and do) shape how they define language teaching and learning. They can become more aware of the impact of their lessons on society and the impact of society on their practice by consciously engaging in critical pedagogy or critical action research, an extension of action research explored as part of the previous stage. After teachers reflect on their philosophy, principles, theory, practice, and beyond practice, they can compile all these for evaluation purposes.

Conclusion

This book outlines one way of implementing or operationalizing reflective practice in TESOL by using a framework for reflecting in five stages: philosophy, principles, theory, practice, and beyond practice. Teachers can use the framework as a lens through which to view their professional (and personal) worlds—what has shaped their professional lives—as they become more aware of their philosophy, principles, theories, and practices, and how these impact issues inside and beyond practice. I believe that such a holistic approach to reflection produces more integrated second language teachers who are self-aware and understand how to interpret, shape, and reshape their practice throughout their careers. The information produced from reflection during each stage can be compiled into a teaching portfolio and used for collaborative teacher evaluation purposes. In such a manner, the teacher is not separated from the act of teaching when reflecting or being evaluated: the teacher *is* the teaching just as the dancer *is* the dance!

References

Abednia, A., Hovassapian, A., Teimournezhad, S., & Ghanbari, N. (2013). Reflective journal writing: Exploring in-service EFL teachers' perceptions. *System, 41*(3), 503–514.

Ashcraft, N. (2014). *Lesson planning.* Alexandria, VA: TESOL International Association.

Bleakley, A. (1999). From reflective practice to holistic reflexivity. *Studies in Higher Education, 24*(3), 315–330.

Crookes, G. (2009). The practicality and relevance of second language critical pedagogy. *Language Teaching, 43*(3), 1–16.

Deng, L., & Yuen, A. H. K. (2011). Towards a framework for educational affordances of blogs. *Computers and Education, 56*(2), 441–451.

Dewey, J. (1933). *How we think: A restatement of the relation of reflective thinking to the educative process.* Boston, MA: Houghton-Mifflin.

Farrell, T. S. C. (2013). *Reflective teaching.* Alexandria, VA: TESOL International Association.

Farrell, T. S. C. (2015). *Promoting teacher reflection in second language education: A framework for TESOL professionals.* New York, NY: Routledge.

Farrell, T. S. C. (2018). *Research on reflective practice in TESOL.* New York, NY: Routledge.

Farrell, T. S. C., & Bennis, K. (2013). Reflecting on ESL teacher beliefs and classroom practices: A case study. *RELC Journal, 44*(2), 163–176.

Farrell, T. S. C., & Ives, J. (2015). Exploring teacher beliefs and classroom practices through reflective practice. *Language Teaching Research, 19*(5), 594–610.

Freeman, D. (2016). *Educating second language teachers.* Oxford, England: Oxford University Press.

Goodson, I. (2000). Professional knowledge and the teacher's life and work. In C. Day, A. Fernandez, T. E. Hauge, & J. Muller (Eds.), *The life and work of teachers. International perspectives in changing times* (pp. 13–25). London, England: Falmer Press.

Kagan, D. M. (1992). Implications of research on teacher belief. *Educational Psychologist, 27*(1), 65–90.

Kanno, Y., & Stuart, C. (2011). Learning to become a second language teacher: Identities-in-practice. *The Modern Language Journal, 95*(2), 236–252.

Kong, M. (2014). Shifting sands: A resilient Asian teacher's identity work in Australia. *Asia Pacific Journal of Education, 34*(1), 80–92.

Lin, W., Shein, P. P., & Yang, S. C. (2012). Exploring personal EFL teaching metaphors in pre-service teacher education. *English Teaching: Practice and Critique, 11*(1), 183–199.

Liu, Y., & Xu, Y. (2011). Inclusion or exclusion? A narrative inquiry of a language teacher's identity experience in the "new work order" of competing pedagogies. *Teaching and Teacher Education, 27*(3), 589–597.

Palmer, P. J. (1998). *The courage to teach.* San Francisco, CA: Jossey-Bass.

Polat, N. (2010). Pedagogical treatment and change in preservice teacher beliefs: An experimental study. *International Journal of Research, 49*(6), 195–209.

Richards, J. C., & Lockhart, C. (1994). Reflective teaching in second language classrooms. New York: Cambridge University Press.

Shi, L., & Yang, L. (2014). A community of practice of teaching English writing in a Chinese university. *System, 42*(1), 133–142.

Waring, H. Z. (2014). Mentor invitations for reflection in post-observation conferences: Some preliminary considerations. *Applied Linguistics Review, 5*(1), 99–123.

Yuan, R., & Lee, I. (2014). Pre-service teachers' changing beliefs in the teaching practicum: Three cases in an EFL context. *System, 44*, 1–12.

Zeichner, K., & Liston, O. (1996). *Reflective teaching: An introduction.* Mahwah, NJ: Lawrence Erlbaum Associates.

Made in the USA
Las Vegas, NV
13 January 2022

41235948R10033